SONNY HALL

The
Blues
Comes
With
Good
News

First published in Great Britain in 2019 by Hodder & Stoughton
An Hachette UK company

A CIP catalogue record for this title is available from the British Library

Illustrations by Jack Laver
Design & Art Direction by Rob Meyers, RBPMstudio

ISBN 978 1 529 38397 3

Printed and bound in Great Britain by Clays Ltd, Elcograf S.p.A.

Hodder & Stoughton policy is to use papers that are natural, renewable
and recyclable products and made from wood grown in sustainable
forests. The logging and manufacturing processes are expected to conform
to the environmental regulations of the country of origin.

Hodder & Stoughton Ltd
Carmelite House
50 Victoria Embankment
London EC4Y 0DZ

www.hodder.co.uk

For my mother Belinda
For Kai
For Knotty
For Dan

1

Fancy being crooked? —

2

Dear Sally, —

Gibberish —

8

4

Skanky Truth —

4

Skanky Truth, Continued —

Introduction

This book is an uncooked confessional note to the world after years of hiding, dispirited, black and familiarly blue . . . all over London . . . accompanied by only blinded dewy eyes and handy manipulation tactics to woooo the world each day, to continue a vicious cycle, of getting what i thought i supposedly needed.

I started writing during my Rehab process over the summer of 2017 and soon came to feel and trust that i could confide in something that was not destructive. Something that was finally more freeing than shattering myself, something that was potent in its unapologetic nakedness, something telling and something far more telling than the spoil of one human being, something to expose whatever was underneath that desperate yearn to be a wrecker, that frantic yearn to marry a different oblivion every single morning, something i only ever knew, coming from a home of violence and drug and alcohol addiction.

Writing has become my way to make sense of living.

My only way to order the now stirring and smashingly sweeping clarity i now possess as a fellow human being within this world.

The Blues Comes With Good News is a collection of sincere poems that have come to life throughout these past 2 years of writing. Poem's given a life by a pen and a forever growing clear head which sometimes is clouded by shenanigans and happenings that occur to all of us humans, through living.

The Blues Comes with Good News chips away at the corrupt meandering that we may all fall into from time to time, due to the state of this wonderful yet skewed world and our attentively searching selfs. Aiming to write gratefully by never filtering one word and always veering to my truth, for the sake of relishing the freeing sensation i need from writing and grafting with the mission of ridding nonsense that i feel, see and hear from day to day.

Always connecting to the reality of the worlds frighteningly warming normality. Always searching for the best spot, to be that fly on the wall or familiarly in the midst of conundrums, through spells of love and favourably, unknown inviting occurrences.

12

This lengthy note is a petrol that pushes a message to never shy away from the truth that will always spring up in other people's doings or your own and with that, finding comfort in simply knowing the correctness of things that may not be correct or feel correct. However as long as it is sincere, i have found, that it will always sway afar from the rubbish that can make us feel down and out.

The Blues Comes With Good News is my healthily unapologetic rationalisation to all that one can think and feel.

Fancy being crooked? —

Tickety Boo

This is far from a trend
You'll just know
Once you're round the bend

Tetanus Nuts and Bolts

This life shy of numbing becomes a pharmacy
True clarity entertains the bank of thrills
Pansy cunt, look now
No pills stomach the same
Remembering names, forgetting half the face
With the pressing cold
Lips insensate
Yet your taste holds it burrow at the tip of my tongue
Dead and drugged
Stomachs still turn
As if the next boy will get snuffed
Roughneck entity
Bell me back
Blooming heck
Life took all I had left
Owed a sack
Crack my back
You're just like smack
Smouldered by adrenalin
I miss my mate Jack
Exploiting gak off the beaten track
City lights reason with the gloomy
All of my love so far has been ever so moody
Shake my hand
The 7th cappuccino bows down to all that's bland
Life with rakish eyes
Tugs the brittle old man
With mirrored pity
I'm courteous
Oh so courteous
In the nook of my city
The 55 bus
Incoherent lust
My minds gone bust
Hush before we are dormant
Showered in dust
Closing down, with many pounds
Just heaving frowns
And a life to re—think

Off the Wagon

Reap reform
Seek idiocy
The rear of the stuffed cafe
Red bricks
Pristine tables
Rich with napkins
The floor could do with a hoover
That fella could have utilized a fucking napkin
Remove fine powder
An overdose of moral fibre
The backbone of proper cleanliness
Was formed by one or two dirty days.

What do You really Want

Sneaky zest gatherer
I see you polishing your cold black heart
With a handkerchief you stole from my right back pocket
Penalise the needy
Reward the seedy
Force feed the greedy
It is all black and white until you start to picture things
And other things as favourable soul cleansing delights
Daytime nightmare dreamer when did it get so bizarre?
Hocus pocus whiskey guzzler discharging fake love
In the back ends of Balthazaar's
Shadow corner
Midnight standstill wanderer
Lick her saving barriers
Starting from her insides
Like snapping a thorn in half
You have to go into the procedure carefully from the rims
A rose needs to protect its dying beauty from people who
pose like impoverished crows leaching on the external
Spitting cotton from their feverish mouths
You were a prick even before you got pricked..
Familiar blood leaks
Don't dismantle or tamper with the already happening
Cunting spastic
Controller of cosmic fantasy
Orgasmic fantastic tragedies

I own the word debauchery
Because i knew of each teething outcome
before you even sought after any kind of achieving creed
Suck my asshole with your luscious mouth
And your tongue like a beehive
Glowing corner
The light smiles at us cheekily
Briefly
Slapping us back to the other corner
Now, tell me
What do you want?

When they Run Out

Our backs pressed to the floorboards
Our limbs deprived of any sensation
For now
We don't have to question all
Blood on the ceiling
Nails dirt ridden and skin peeling
Self effacing mirrors become the walls
For now
Beauty comes last within this constant stupefied mode
We are more than happy to fall
Daisy vacates the room to usher us some more
The bin bags are gushing
My loves demon's are blushing
The pupils of your eyes scaringly precise
Surrounded by a glacier of dishwater ice
In this dreary room
We entertain the same lifeless motions
Humdrum scum
Plodding emotion
Daisy, please....
The turkey is getting cold.

I Know a Trickster or Three

My endeavours off the Gloucester Road
Failed to match the surroundings
Smack clowning
My current clobber may need some nifty rounding
Droopy smirks
Ejaculates starry eyed slobber
Dripping
Stooping to my clobber
I will not coincide until the clock works
My blocked nose wasn't to know otherwise
I am a living representation of the clerks loose tie
A pen pusher in variant ways
White lies
With an usher for Waifs and Strays
Gloucester Road

Holds my internal brabble
While 6 o'clock traffic folds
With a cursory babble
I sit
Governed by the curb
Hurting to muster a sole word
Each attire that is
Draped
Worn and clenched
By limbs
Repeats
Like a recap of a mishap
Hearts n' souls in a trap
Chameleons with their tastes on loan
Some would say
Each to their own
Twined by a cunning load
Really n' Truly
I'm torn to conform to trends
That bend
My already hellbent moral codes

London Spits out Desperate Charmers

Riddle mimed cravings
Stumper perky takings
I heard
Saturday's day holds surplus fortune

Today
Someone mentioned that today is Tuesday

Waiting
Scraping
Mostly taking
Scratching your balls might pass the time
Surely satisfying the itch is a Buddhist crime
Most monks love to do so
Letting go
Letting rubbish nip at ya soul
Addictive punishing crack whoopee Yo—Yo
Meditative pick pocket
Pocket 2 lover's constipated desire
Pocket 23 Nitrous Oxide canisters
Therefore a couple boneheads doomed forged laughters
Pocket inauthentic praise splattered with cringe imagined vomit
Wash your hands Sir
Then propel and pickpocket
Pocket the fixed sickness that any poem can rid
Pocket the swollen aching ape like trampoline like tonsils that you
carved out of your own mouth
Then pick pocket a good man's healthy life sized tonsils
You're on the road to good health Sir
I promise
I'm honest
Trust me

Savvy hand fidget
Get ya needs
Get ya needs
Oi Boy!
Oi Oi know the craft of ya new found giving toy!
Fidget hands Oi!
PICK POCKET
Pocket 269 caterpillars sleeping in their cocoons
I've sadly tried to catch butterflies my entire life
Pocket the freeing prick that a sincere poem will give
Pocket other's valuable shrapnel
Pocket that hazel eyed petticoat and leave her heart on the table as
she'd do yours
Pocket each unaffected step of his and hers final dance
Pocket hope

Pocket the next man's loss
Pocket any seaside towns depression
And create a woe bound story from the good news of the blues
Pocket the delusion of fame and wank over your own name
Pocket a switchblade
Pocket dib dab sherbets rack it up n sniff the cunting stuff
Pocket all that is in the back pocket's of the king's servants
Pocket it!
PICK POCKET IT!

Adoration headbutting nothingness
Plucked countless kindling hoping hopers
Hope to be the very spark that chokes unmolested emptiness
Hope to be rich
Poor of nonsense
Poor of spoil
Steal the best things
Steal the things that people ravage over
The things that make people kick the bucket over
For absolutely zero
Just one defeated hero

In the Madhouse

In the Madhouse
Stray dogs potter while ignoring one and other
Orphans feed each other filling sobs lovingly
In the Madhouse
Tumbleweed accumulates on the masters bed
In the Madhouse
The Master is fed up
Of all that is said
Done
And laughed about
Politicians are seen as diseased ticks
Or even septic dicks
That stand with the look of devilry
The Master is dishevelled
In the Madhouse
The animation of typical living is non existent
The Master is a phoney
A naive failed doctor
Who's own life depicted him
Like the surgeon he once hoped to be
The Master is a swindler
In the Madhouse
The act of being is dwindled
The abandoned peter out
Little by little
Humans are splintery
In the Madhouse
A bottle is insecure in the wrong mans hand

Lorimer Street Regression

After hours
The other night in Brooklyn
I kissed a girl that was infatuated with my old friend Charlie
The roof of my mouth went numb
Fueled by lust
Later
Diluted and stimulated
By the tonic of one ladies after midnight ritual
As an ex-cokehead
I welcomed contrary of intimacy at this point
Blurting an altered sensation
With shooting pains
Down each terrorized lane of my veins
The girl smiles at me with a telling comfort

I Am
What I Need

23 harassed chocolate bar wrappers
Plastic comfort
Someone finally acknowledged that my trousers were
hugging my ankles
My doctor often claps his giving palms
I click my fingers when I'm hopeful
Soon I'll be a pill
Soon I'll be able to piss pills
Soon I'll be able to shit pills
Make sure that the box is made from ebony wood

The Closest Thing
to Heartfelt Justice

Here is one of the cunts that came before
Strung up from his shitstained boxers on a flagpole
Above his cheating father's grave
I penetrate the cunts sheepish solemn eyes with mine
While my right arm is wrapped around a lady he once knew rather well
A lady he once made love to
While slimey reservations were stashed up his asshole
My left arm now cups her breasts
While I look the cunt in his eyes
Then back to the effusive correlation of mine and her's sparkly dimes
I wouldn't want to burden this cunt with heartfelt vivid
memories of me and his old lady
Wrestling oozing emotion
Like cracked out swans with our motions
An easy loving equation splashing full admiration
But then again I want to be a teacher to all the cunts
that think its savoury being overhasty
And shady
I have caught a butterfly for the very first time
Eventually people's greed will die
Mostly involuntarily

Writing Content

Tonight
I fondled with a 53 year old lady
And all I could think about
Was writing this

OCD Disorder

I could do many things in an orderly fashion
Guzzle a bottle pronto
Much opiates like cheerios
And dance with the terror in love
All this done on the table top
In an orderly fashion
Outspoken gimmicks follow the shared hank-a-chief
Swirling flem
And knocking teeth
Within a kiss
Morphin revolt
Sadly they can't miss this
They
The classist's
I have under my fingernails
My scumbag trail
I gently entail
Scoping limelight
Morbidly
Yet orderly
Dancing in a fight
Seeking a worthy shiner
Tonight
On the table top
Order is scally like
Order
Is a pear
Yet to be ripe

I am Normally Sluggish and Crooked

With the blue moon
We are grudgingly receiving consent
To acknowledge saturday's noon
On a day you are torn to breathe
The effort of morphing into a slug
Your subtle ease to own a fooling service
Your need to receive
Gloopy porridge
This morning your fingers smell familiarly peculiar
The shy water under the Williamsburg bridge
Moulds tranquility
Subtly balancing dismissed confusion
And the innocent madness
Of the towering merged red and brown bricks of the East River
Decades of poor misfits
Licking societies balls
Just to merely fit
In the trick of all that is
Everyone unknowingly holds the burrow
Of life's incognito tick
Tearing through moisturised skin
Exploiting the fine line
Between a gentlemen's values
And his wayward sins
In my circle of crooks
We indulge in our stolen books
Binging on mischief
Downtown
With little sound

Just chattered teeth
Planting seeds in the hope of love
To lead a furthered hug
Tugging me
The bent slug
Through Chinatown and all around
Cracked red paint
Glossy Catastrophes
Smacked beings with no sake
Our minds the factories
Of post murder fleas
Bloody mysteries
And the delusional blueprint
To harbour the bees knees

Parisian Lube

Meet me at Le Select in Paris
Where I don't pay for the coffee
Nor the food
Notoriety and sickness
Hand in hand
2 years ago here
I welcomed many weak handshakes
Each green bleeding morning
Teething codeine
Through weathered charm and confident English
Puzzling the French pharmacists
My made up chest infection
Afar from realities actual sickness
Was a successful harboured lie
Just like Lily Allen in her prime
Numbing meant sweet unmeasured harmful business
Blacklist the English fella
Paris enabled any hopeless mans plan
Horny for destruction
Dismantling care
Forging dummy romance
All this
Close to normality with many magic bullets in my stomach
Parisians hate everyone
Parisians hate themselves

Habitual London
Habitual me

Stumbling down the stairs
To look up and see deaths stare
Milking a habit in London
Well
Would ya say flighty?
Swell?
Never so slightly
Like a rabbit
I spring through London beared by my habit
Elastic and fantastic
I may as well smoke plastic
District line
Line
Gloucester road
20 Benzos
12 Vicodin
Belated sins
My pennys never win
Maybe so
Why i settled for Echo Falls And not
Exquisite gin
Who muttered?
I muttered
No recall
To thread a thought
That 2 more pills won't sting
Im back
Oblivion's trap
Holloway
Hackney
I can't go back

This Food Tastes like Shit and this Money in my Back Pocket gives Me the Bloody itch — The Dorchester

Successful alarm
When did your saving sound resign?
Oh no
Oh yes
Oh no
Oh yes
Glamour on
Blinkers on
Gloves on
Me and my lover
just shattered a bottle of Juglar Cuvee at The Dorchester
And i spat on my lovers red gory steak
Before she engulfed lukewarm death
Then i polished my whacked shoes with a blemished napkin
After wiping my ass
With the tissue my lover used to smear her tears
All from her face and from the table top
Oh yes
I have money now and i couldn't feel more death hungry
I don't have a clue why my lover is crying
She has everything

But me
Whoever wants to look at us will get admitted to hospital
to visit their own broken shrewd self's
Snap me and my lover into 33 exposed pieces
through one honest gaze   37
Accidents do happen
Frostbite indoors can happen
Frail structures here we go again
The dessert wine has arrived and also the Gruyere cheese
I look to my grubby toes for guidance
While questioning the nasty finish on the hardwood veneer flooring
Should we eat the cheese before the wine or the wine before the
cheese?
Or should we mix and match all at the same time?
Oh no
Here we go again
Fortune pollutes the simplicity of one's sterilized brain
Me and my lover don't know what to do with it all
Scallywags with money
We are the ones that phlegm on things that glimmer
Then pocket it all to overshadow the smirking muggy winner
Confusion in contentment
An overt prisoner cannot except freedom so easily
Like us with all of these nice things
All of these nice things
Why does everyone happily leak blood to be a winner?

Sinking

To sink one drink
To the next
To gladly think slowly killing myself
Was best
My sick reasoning
Could
Float any boat
Knowing
I've nearly burnt the toast
This fine cocktail
Not to boast
Tells a stirring saga
Of the fact that I'd rather
Sink this boat
So far from this coast
While
I happily heighten my dose

Everyone Should Hate Themselves

I was the only traveller
On the Overground
To place shrapnel in the lost lady's pot
It's a lot
To identify with hurt in a fellow
And to simply carry on
The evening's trot

The sniveling momentary catch that our eyes buried
Zapped me of any thought of Sally
Any thought to be merry
Any trust in the thumping hearts
That surrounded me

Scrappy nag float bitterly
Outsiders dance arrogantly
Empathy swallowed
Before it's shaken and served neat
Gastric acid
What continuously vibrates human beings with hateful shudders?
Embryos the legendary campaign of innocence

Battersea
Tenderly Batters Thee

Battersea Mister
With loose flesh grazes of the knee
An upright swayed smirk flaunting cheek
Telling a future court case or three
Battersea Missy
Tongue and escapism squeeks
Market working father
She'd much prefer her love neat
Perhaps her jaded side
Would much prefer
Her love crude and wrestling with sweet
Top hat
Sack a bow tie
The first button left untouched
In youth little speaks too much
Tasteless environments
Smutty acquaintances
In youth burning desire smothers all rational
Even soppy love coated trust
Both Battersea Heads
Have best attended the party of the survivors fury
Where the Judge and the Jury
Chose their alined day of absence
Certitude is a tragic skill
We often hope with lathered palms
We often choke on the dewy eyed aperture of societies qualms
Battersea's raised alarms
Chizzles husky willpower
And strapping stamina
Worth a future kings ransom

This earth,
The Petrol Station for
All of us Fidgeters

At this point
It would be ignorant to not write about the Fidgeters petrol
Acknowledging the number of sweaty handshakes exchanged in these
last 20 years
Gratefully taught me of the artful fact of portioned unease
that stands on humanities throat
Hands on hips
Cum on tits
She said "Acknowledge my clit, i don't want to ever come back from
this!!"
Escapist lippy lip
Some time ago i knew of a italian lady who ate 1 meal every 2 days
When she did eat, it was of vegan rubbish
She didn't tell anyone of her age
She was drunkenly possessive over people that half cared for her
actuality
I loved her and i thought she was a great human
But i'm a ignorant sensitive englishman
Imagine 2 lost dogs from 2 different countries
Trying to calm each other down
By searching for a suitable hole to place a forgettable desire
She never in her days consumed a drop of alcohol
She crawled like a smacked frail cat around London
Clawing at pretty people
Bleeding blurred topics
Showcasing her needy misanthropic brain
Kissing the bankers

Wanking the wankers
Blowing young men who were still figuring it all out
Young men who felt like they were maturing from her grooming
company
Blossoming but dying slowly
Never meeting blooming comfort
Or any connection with the unreal puppets she drew her life from
Discomfort dictating every heartbeat
Blossoming in sickness
Blossoming with ridiculousness
Last tuesday on Borough Market
My wise mate Jim strictly ordered her to learn to adore the glue in
honey
Not the sweetness
He also said to treasure the fizz in your belly from champagne
Not the drunken tizzy bubbling up your brain
Shake my hand
If you are constantly dizzied by the great sting of life

Back to this lady
Some lady
Once my dear lady warm to me like gravy
The last time i saw her she had one shoe on
And she was blowing on a white flute
Somewhere on Charlotte Street
Staring hopefully into a drain that sat just past her ten toes

Trying to Forget About Ritzy Shit in Notting Hill is a Mug's Game

It's toilsome remembering
Next to me
2 gentlemen
Gently
Chatting about qualms of
A half a million pound loan
Their hardship holds a dishonest moan
Like a prick from a cactus
I float
Buffered
Like paint to a canvas
Trying to forget
Today's anguish

Is it the Drugs I Abstain from (Barcelona)

Pinch yourself with a plastic bag
Over your head
I may need to do so
The bag
My bag
Draped over the chair beside me
Fooled one
Out of squinted eyes
A quick assumption came to my surprise
For a second
Or 3
The bag
Appeared as a human being to me

Me n' Jack

Lick my bottle
Pull my throttle
Red muck
This liquid stuff
Hurt idiocy becomes our motto
To steal or to borrow?
Heros today
Fools tomorrow
Fasten my buckle
Heighten my chuckle
Fuel my wronged hustle
Join my questionable tustle
Kicked in the mouth by a horse
Money
Little remorse
Shoulder by shoulder
Double—dealing breaks the sealing to our gluttony
In these 24 hours
You are my winner

Hectic Affection on Percy Street

I fell in love with a lady on Percy Street
Who shon shy light upon the gypsy in me
Tightening my screws
The imposters horses fell rambling to the blues
The sky's colours for the first time
In living
Came to life
Water acquired rich taste
Earth's soil laid lovebeds throughout London
Dust vanished
Cupid's blood boiled
Fleeing pain
My pores toiled
I keep slashing my left arm with my pen
To embrace some reality
And love still shows
No matter how much blood will still flow

The Front Door and The Cobbled Floor

Sick oblivious oblivion.

I keep pacing to the same front door, to purchase these circular tablets.

An almost naive exchange with a fooling service.

This mews off Cromwell Road sure does know the bottom of
my worn Oxford brogues.

Hurried greetings.

After I reach the front door, I disregard the human being.

In the dimness of this daily minute or so chit chat or liaison shall we say..

Well whatever phrase deters any given reality to these everlasting exchanges.

Beating around the bush.

In this obscurity,

I pocket my circular things.

Wealthy eyes gawp through double glazed windows.

I think so anyway.

The front door shuts and I already forgot what the giving
human being muttered.

The world is shallow when I am tied to these circular things.

I want to spit on the cobbles in descredit to all i have trusted to love.

But, I'll need that saliva...

Dry swallowing is a task.

Confusion landslide...

I have gained time to nab a drink, grappling with confusion,
baffed to even think.

Another thought intrudes...

How on earth, am I at this front door on a swanky mews in Chelsea
when I was born into the dampness of drugs and violence, in Essex.

I do like the front door.
It is rather alluring, there is definitely something.
Plus, the cobbles seem to adore me.
They accommodate every stride I take.
My Oxford brogues, gliding, evenly.
Hats off to these stones.
I think the things have hit now.
Any shuddering or rancid flinching has fled.
Instead, love.
Instead, I am no longer deprived of a way.
Harmless ways.
I just know that this won't stay.
I'll be back.
Back to the front door.
And my tattered Oxford brogues...
Back,
Back on the cobbled floor.

Whoever Makes the Rules Should get Ransacked to the Point of Gasps

There is a peculiar sound that births from our gob's when we stretch
Humans
I have a 20 dollar bill in my breast pocket and I'm in London
Why do americans cry if they don't get granted a tip?
Cretins
There is a certain sound that penetrates a mans lips when we cum
Humans
I was told I couldn't gamble because of a high risk of
losing my future home
A triangle has more sex appeal than a square
My absent old man told me to never give your time of day to a square
I'd vouch for a homeless man over a city worker
I was told that I have a mental illness
Doesn't everyone cut the labels from the clothes that they buy?
Authorities intice terror
To some
Moody living comes smoothly like italian leather
I was told I had to go to university
Haha

Feeling Good

I feel good with lunatics.
Pipe dream days sheepish of a fix...
I am keen to be the monkey degenerate.
Today I am most definitely eager and ravenous to plunge my fingers
in a few more pies.
In my dining room, vibrant looneys surround the table for a feast of ideas.
Ideas stemmed from the roots and fruits of suffering.
Shall I mention that we do not eat cherries here.
We eat nothing.
On this table I am digesting my very own bluffing, while every other
fellow is huffing and puffing on something that'll hand you a rumpling
of harmony, something like an eighth heaven...
Smothered by a heavy hearted army.
One hit and the table flips.
Opaque tears drip confidently from the marble eyes of my crazy Daisy,
perched next to me.   51
I feel good with my honey.
Almost.
In another days mind the act of claiming you feel good is almost match-
ing to blaming your lowered voice on the disagreeing weather.
Odd balls are a touch of tonic to my day.
If you are an avid...
You know the word...
Well...
If you are an avid...

Worldly saviour
Worldly samaritan
A fairy with a loud ish voice
Well...
Hats off to you.

Here we are one sandwich short of an indoor picnic.
We bought the food for your butchered thoughts.
We make one and other feel good through practiced distortion of souls
that fought to receive far less than nought.
One hit and table flips.

Dear Sally, —

You know
What Love is

Weasel worm
Cut the slime
Sniggling other
Pluck the spillage
Blushing anger tipping any upright wit within this
This flipping abyss leaking bliss to twist
Ya know what
I'd rather rot
No explaining true admiration when scalding frustration
Burns linked palms
Melting tease
Tickle me please

Your Sweetness

The sweetness you bear
Seeps right in
Behind closed doors
I swear this loves within
The sweetness you bear
Floods all that's bitter
Me
Myself
And
I
The dosey dud
Nothing but a loved up mug
That's almost a July's night sky
I picture you way up high
Too far from my eyes
See
Im quickly absent
For my respect to you
Is harmless to few
And
Hopeless to some
I'm the result
Of a angry son
And a junkie mum
So now
I question all my love that's to give
Soon
Oh
Soon
I hope my love is to give
Im adjacent to you
As your sweetness seeps through
Tell me

What do we do?

Hoping to Grip Soap

Hope to me
Is like
Gripping soap to me
Your potency is close to me
It's happening
To hang on your hope
Is like
Putting my neck round a rope
What hope?
Now i wonder what soap to wash with
Our little myths
Runs through this rusty sieve
Now
I wonder
To go
Or
To live
This hope
This soap

You Heighten Separation

Detachment at height of sweet nothings
Discrete brain wanders
Setting apart the pudding from the very start
Betting actuality to be cared for like china
Minus a saving remark
Your destruction
Not your empathy
Hissing gentle offers off the telepathy of admiration and a painkiller
One more
Fall to my floor
Stick your foot in my door
Your governing hierarchy of things
Things that hover
Kissed by zesty tingles
And grappled by obsessions that mingle
Thing's not to be named
Never come as a single
Mourish
Unhitched
What's the sum of you with a prick but no riddles?
A lousy nick
Alienation
Slit
And split

If Death is not Lurking then any Kind of leisure Surely is Not

This lady had something hidden under her bed
Something to bloody a man under her covers
It's something to feel such a thing
Everything gone
Everything lost to paranoia and the death of 2 straggling candle lights
Everything lost to the misunderstanding of a crooked fraternity
Everything has already been pummelled red
Angels have sex too
But angles don't wish death upon anything
Anything can be perceived as a threat
When you're constantly tickling adrenalines balls
I wonder where she hid the knife
Soft skin right before the brittle asshole
Spreading fingertips over cursed limbs
And damp crevices
We are hot butter smothered on toasted ciabatta
Liquid sludge
Body scum to splatter
Racing mad hatter
Daggering matter
I do not want you to murder me but something tells me
it wouldn't really matter
Hate masked by adoration bleeding filthy inflictions that lather
I do not want to die in a lifeless flat above Sainsbury's
on Portobello Road
She said " What do you want?"

I want less of the stuff that captivates less than one emotionless face
Less of the stuff that co signs oblivion in room 203
at the cunting Chiltern
Less of the stuff that enables idiotic human beings to
present soulless handshakes
Less of the stuff that sits proudly behind wrong doers,
myself and her majesty the queen
Oh and also those validation sniffing deluded dainty
no good phone scrollers
That have thoughtful and sometimes vigorous sex
with their telephones every morning at 3AM
Less of this lady sat next to me
Who is smoking all of my dear cigarettes
nd strangling me every 14 minutes
As a dreadfully optimistic grandiose plan to pump
blood into my cock
I looked at my sorry boxers shrivelled up on her meaningless floor
Her meaningless walls spoke of some meaningless life
I turned off her lights to feel otherwise

Hello Strawberry

Hello Strawberry
I just might
Take a bite
Before you are ripe
For I devour
All that's sour
This meet and greet
Medling sweet
And
A humble questionable cower
So I'll find my feet
Just after I eat

Wedded to a
Losing Illusion

It is never ever what it is cracked up to be
Fantasy is far from clever
Disillusionment becomes the queen bee
At present
Im sheepish to conform
To a little nudge
Even a graze
For I'm fleeing this crippling daze
Butterfly
Oh the ploy of your elated cocoon
Squeezing my interior
While pulling my limbs
To the seizing moon
I thought one day
To bloom
Well
I fancied to
My pie in the sky in cuckoo land
Teared rain drizzles clearly
I touched the rainbow
Just so
Nearly

63

Containing me

My budding interest for a fantasy
Not to be obtained
Keeps me far from contained
A off reason to take a chance
Then
To wonder why she wouldn't take the dance
I'll shy away
But
Offer my best glance
A sick beat
Could
Find any cheats feet
Nonetheless
Ignore my cheek
I'd rather be contained
Not sane
Just contained
You give me a reason to chew harder
And ruin myself faster
Hidden by the laughter
I'm all gone
Thereafter
Thanks for polishing my brain
Saying my name
Noticing I'm pained
Yet
I'm still contained

That Night Made me Leak

Melancholy looms
Fingers bind and fret
Palms lather
Lips crisp
No kisses will gather
Your body a ladder
As if this
Melancholy actuality
Doesn't really matter
Tell me
Because I'm breathless
I wish
To be in your bee hive mind
Tell me
Because I see less
I wish to receive
A kind helping
Through the acknowledgment
Of debauched eyes
Eyes meet
Married and weak
Your eyes make me leak
How can I lie
How can I cry
When I have your eyes
Behind gloomy skies

The Way you Taint me

I'm noticed
I have been noted
I'm a sticker
Some kind of leaning prick
To you
I'm bitter
I'm besotted
I'm preoccupied
With a yearn to hide
Without being snide
I'm taken
I'm mistaken
I'm devoted
I'm besotted
I'm trusted
I'm a broken pen
I'm busted
I'm obsessed
Im love, when love is crack and I'm crack
When that deluded fella thought crack was smack
I'm the one you want back
I'm a mishap
I'm my own trap
I'm a fracture
A fraction of you
I'm good news singing
And with you
I'm muted
With you
I'm polluted

For Now I am Not Deluded

For now, I haven't heard from you.
For now, well I hope, for now.
For now, I haven't drank a gallon of bleach.
For now, well I hope, for now.
For now, I haven't accidentally slit my throat while doing
a fine shape up... A Sweeney Todd job.
For now, well I hope, for now.
For now, I haven't plunged down the stairs and snapped
my leg in 3 places, then overdosed on the pain meds they
gave me to put on my toast.
For now, well I hope, for now.

Clutching Pens

Until we touch again
I'll ponder on thoughts to mend
I wonder who taught me to pretend
Until our words meet again
I'll simmer on what could be
Gutting laughter
And happiness
Here after
I'll hope to find my pen
By this point
I've thought on the thought of you
Fermenting my seed
I've bought a dozen pens now
Yet you haven't came to be

Doped.

Is this just fascination
Because I quite like fascination
Butter will melt between us
Eyes will spill
Fascination holds little time
Just dim witted signs
My lips arid
After yours im buttered
No longer dry
In fascination
I'm married to a deadline
Settled
As you carelessly water my petals
Sometimes parched
Because in the haze of fascination
Only wishing imagination
Departs

Don't be a Stranger

I used to wear love as a loose garment
Now I bathe
I bathe behind your blue glare
Now I'm laced
Laced vigorously
Laced with tantalizing danger
To show a stranger attention
Was a no go
I promise you that
I used to
Now
This stranger
Is my only affection
My dear affliction
And my cared for addiction
I still gape
For one was swollen
A long while after
One was stolen
But still holding
Grasping at despair
Behind your blue glare
I'm a stranger to you
Through and through
It's like
Turned backs
Stapled frowns
Damp dressing gowns
And a unbothered danger of death sign
Sat next to inviting flowers
Strangers could utter the bare minimum
Yet
What makes us strangers is subliminal

I Merely want
You around

Let me find shelter in your fondness
Let me escape silently
I cannot fuel any love without a chase
No sweet face
No available place
Can be the remake
Of the dynamic where I was replaced
I search for a love so manic
In my eyes so magic
A specific demise
Came with no surprise
A dose of available love is well kept
Yet
Quickly swept
To love typically
Well
I'd say
I'm inept
So My Lovely
Watch how you step
Don't say you love me
For you may kinder
Regret

Maybe you should
See me Out

Crushed
Pinched
Tweaked
Burst open to be scrutinized in awe
As high regards seeps
Maybe
Spoken through a tribute
Of spit plopped in all that it is you eat
Ohhhh what a beauty
A real treat
Rare delicacies in the realm of people that have been shelled
Unattended children yelled
Desire is building
Feeling to a sensation
If I keep going I won't see my pension
Warmth topped by concern
Steals my best turn
Not to mention
My lessons that will burn
Touching a flame
Springs the hooligans out of me
That other mister can merely try and interpret all I see
Fire and desire
Excuses not a single sausage
Tell ya new mister
I'll smoulder him to a walking blister
Lady lover
I'm tired to shove
I'm tired to whisper
Just why this mister
Lady lover
I'm tired to love
I cradle my expiry
Like the off food you were so looking forward to eat
Now you've missed your treat

The lump in my throat
Is the note to our doting
Seamless breaths
Between a kiss
Some so revolting
Lick my cheek
And help me reminisce You
We
I
You are missed
Nude
Seed
Sighs
Crude is missed
Break the pill
Drowsy and ill
Our doting was once real
I'm sick for you
Piss on my face
For our love is replaced
By a hateful taste
Married to lustful haste
I am your waste
I am a scarce trace
Of your treacly paste
To further the chase
We cemented my hearts place
In your fuck face
Poisoned veins
Feed into desires pain
Valued dirt
Dissolves the leisure
In hurt
But only your dirt
Thanks for the lump
You burdened me with a friskful hump
Now
No window is seductive to jump
Because I have you
To hump

74

Humping You
Doting You

Who is that Boy Mimicking Love

Who is that fucking slimey desperate cunting boy?
Please him
Please
As no one will do so
Lights repel and dim
When he enters the room
So please him
Please
As no one else will do so
Who is that pleading, kneeling, needing, yawping, silly,
clumsy existence of a boy?
Dance a dirty tango with him
As heads bow decently to the foiling floor
Lights repel and dim
You can tell
He's never been here before
Feed him the worlds fruits
As you cannot offer him any kind of sincere sweetness
Yourself
Just please him
Please
As no one else will do so
Who Is that boy?
Fancying love
Mind raping love
Mimicking love
Bickering with love
Shooting blanks at love
Starved by love
Booking a table at La Gavroche for love
Chewing Gum for love
Chewing Hydrocodone for love
Doing economical prostitutes for love
Dove watching for love
Shoot me in both knee caps
I'd rather write about Sally

Most Afternoons

I draw a naked lady on my palm
and press her against my cheek
With doting sincerity
No lady has ever felt this passion
This devotion
Nor this closeness
Never
If imagination flipped to reality
Once a day
For 3 flighty seconds
We would still all be searching
And dead

Bewitched by Mucky Things

I wouldn't wanna be ya
Smoked salmon on soggy ciabatta
Your old man a right violent mad hatta
30 compacted sickening bollock bruising bellitting worries
You trust fund kids are unworthy of any life
Burning homes

Nobody shreds a single worry for ya
Scatty light bulbs
Scatty skitzophrenic
With more love than most
Charcoal toast
Less of a mind to boast
Lovely skatty intercourse
There's now blood on my cock
And it's a right fucking rock
Bloody flooded treasured intimacy
And Missy swallows up my peaked heart
I'm now looking for a wedding ring
I still wouldn't wanna be ya
The fat lady never really sings to ya
Even if it's 127 profiteroles that you bring to her
Sourpatch Be my zebra crossing
My sweet crunchy malteser
Nowt to match
But I do surely need ya
Soppy sloppy teaser
I still really wouldn't wanna be ya

Lug a mug off a Cliff Edge, Then you're Sorted

Muggy mugs love a fucking tug
Bed sheets still smell of that smell
The next cheat is keen
To dwell in transparent lies
While he dosses around with undone flies
True eyes shall file that
And some more
Yes

Actual proper mugs
Simmer with zest for each other
Breeding blaggy mugs
A smug thief of my lover
Pissed pants
Polar opposites of many thanks
At first
I had to be drugged and nursed
To not think this was a crude prank
Coolness sank
Under the tank of lava
What a muggy palava
Under this roof
Fantasies of a known hoof
Addressing a noted tooth
Anger shouldn't and wouldn't disclose this fuckerie
Situated me in a far away booth
Solitude to fit one's mood
And a live chainsaw to roar in one's ear
Pills near
Gin clear
Cupids banished

And the judge watching caringly
Drizzled by a blazing horse radish
Petrol Bombs
Confident Thongs
And Anna Domino whistling a tune
Your wish
Noted
Besotted
In agony
Mugs bloom
Mugs have began to shadow me
Mugs
Tugs
Hated like bugs
Despised
Resented
Tie my tie tight
Or use it as a handy noose
By the end of this
Muggy night

Argyle Street
Confessions

Doom and gloom diarrhoea
Sniff the grey air
Meddle with fond admissions
Lick this door knob clean
Bubbly hotel room cell
Dwell just outside of me
The pale city mashes her into
purple and blue liquid zeal
Casting a bruise
and smutty tongues tangling
behind the grey lips of fibbing smitten schmoozes
This is an honouring
To every innocent saboteur
To every hushed love ballad
To this unannounced disclosure

On the 9th floor
She smudged
'I love you'
On the hotel window
For lips to repeat
We drained blood
In pleasure and decency
Flashy jewels for 2
Blurting hot dear intimacy
Her pink perky ovaries spilled red gloop
Over my rock cock
and all over the once vanilla cast bedding
And I love her
I really do love her

Can You Feel
The Wildfire?

WHY WOULD YOU LET THE HOUSE BURN?
I'd kill my favourite human just to sit in this house
This house the sanctuary for fascinated wordy mites and lazy tongues
Free and ready to manipulate the world and any given language
With wobbly productive hands
In love with pens
Not humans
This close to human lady sunk in the centre of my bed
Like a soggy deflated balloon
She looked at my burning house in horror
Why do you write poetry she said, it is so so stupid
I looked at her alien self as she set off a blazing avalanche inside of me
You are so so so stupid i said
I wish you burned to a merely pardoned crisp
You, not the house
You stupid so n so
How could you say such a thing
You may as well stand with racists and hairy bigots
You may as well be all the things i'd get in trouble for saying
And if they would have published it
I would have said it right here
And i'd tell your estranged family too so there would be no chance of
them ever coming back to you
You should burn
You should pleasure yourself with my broken pen from yesterday
I have plenty more
Maybe stuff it up your backside
Now be on your way
Im sat in my house with my published book
And it is all burning to smithereens
I wish it was easy to read something else
Someone else
Instead i am closed
On the other side of an inviting fire
Words melting my soul
Oh delicious poetry

Kissing A Prostitute

— Barcelona

I once thought to save the whole wide world
Because each human eye holds a motionless riot
I kissed a prostitute
And asked her if she was okay
We cradled one and other and spoke of her dead mother and father
Her boss's home address
The nearest place to buy a machete
Her love for drawing and painting
Her happiness
Her daily consumption of cocks and other things
Her journey from Chile to Barcelona
And the similarities in our childhood
Her unobstructable obsession with poetry
Her hate for Mr. Charles Bukowski
Her sickening love for her 3 children
And the fact she would have left this whole entire place by now
if it wasn't for them

Withdrawals

To remain in this puzzle is like trying to kiss you
With a muzzle
I loiter upon a wish
Waiting on a wandering star
Withdrawing from devotion
You're so far
You're stuck to me like tar
You're my sun lotion
My treasured potion

Now you're really just a poem of mine
The to and fro motion held my heart
Under the line
Now I'm withdrawing from devotion
Loaded with a pine
Crumpled papers
Rattled through a charge
Wines seduction has never had this much charm

A narrowed gist
Engulfed my core
And played my alarms
With my heart on a lead
I forgot all that's to harm

Hundreds of my poems show their concern to you
For no longer
As this loving conundrum is now through
No ink wasted
Just my hearts taste is
Forever misplaced
I found you moorish like strawberry laces
You're a burst of hiccups
A tickling — cough
Through withdrawals
The other lady is far from enough.

Do not Scoot

Even the night creepers run from you
We exist on each end of a hallway at some house in South London
Shake me up
Even Lonesome Larry runs from you
And you have all of it
The unconditional scares of wholesomeness
The medicine we all yearn
You allow me to drop the battering ram
I use on my own home
I'm peaking through the peep hole
And all of our nourishing promises are shattering
Rid sickness
Please
Pretty please
Let go of my gut
Butter me up
Even runty blunt cunts run from you
And you have all of it
The dominion to sway stapled beliefs
The smile that impedes likely souls
Dazzling eyes that only blink to the floor
My marbles to yours
Polka dots always read a toll
The hallway walls suddenly shrivel
Swamping joint withdrawal
I cannot near you
The hallway greatly showed me to the back door
Even love runs from you

Untitled (important)
— Scanned

I've become a bruiser to self
All to not lose her

Forgetting myself

I'm Going to this Pretty Place Now

The top of everyone's list
It is presented as it should
But received how I wish I could
It's never too far away
I lean
And
I sway
Hoping it to be that way
I surprise myself
To my dismay
I'm going to this pretty place now
Where i don't care to know
Where my highs bring lows
And I wouldn't know
This pretty place
Comes with a chase
For the chase
Makes me loose
Like my shoe lace
As I struggle to keep with your pace
This pretty place
Can exploit
Can consume and resume
My very heartache
It's no mistake of mine
That I adore this pretty place
I am a chaser
And nothing can replace her

Sincere Contentment

You're like the cigarette i regret smoking
But still smoke
You're like custard
I could eat you and eat you, choke and be sick
and still eat you
You're like death
You intrigue me and i think about you all the time
You scare me and i don't know when you will arrive
You're an excuse to fleet with fantasy
When i realise
You're like rain to a family picnic
You're like dessert to a fat person
I feel guilty to have you
I'm like a broken middle aged man
And you're my new second hand toy
You're like polished love that makes me spew
You're a walking distinction

You're God
You're something i cannot believe in
You're everything
You're hope in cancer
You're a life enhancer
You're like snot
Everyone loves to look at you in disgust
But in the darkness of solitudes shadow
they would all eat you up
You're sex in the morning
You're meaning
You're a cold touch besides uproar steaming
You're like the world to a newborn baby
You're a terminal illness
You're my verve for life
You're morphine
You're my fourth hydrocodone
You're that article that made me sick after reading it
But i've told the whole world about you
You're like a summer swim in the Thames
You're like two smitten paranoid schizophrenics
trying to figure eachother out

You're dust in the hoover
Where are you gonna go?
You're page 48 in this book
Page 52
Oh and also 66
You're the Devil's relishing fix
You're like piss on snow
You're every poet's dream
You harbour thirty stray faces in one
You carry a gun and can only explore sincere fun
When you point it at yourself
For everyone to watch in trauma
You have wet dreams about exploiting other people's comfort
You're a living reaction of the world's existence
You're destructive each day of the week except for monday
Because that is my job on monday
You're a luxurious chemist offering no advice
Just free rest bites and opiods to loosen my odium for life
You're honey and i'm the buzzy bee
You're the scrambled fuckery everyone wants to take part in
You're the crazy gypsy i've rampaged the whole earth for
You're better than Sally
You're the reason i always wanted more
Well not now
You're a living climax
You're all the world's gold to a suicidal gold miner
You're a bleeding masterpiece
Even the most atrocious artist could make blood diamonds out of you
You're my only purpose
You're death in the post
You're the thing i nearly got to
So so close
A tizzy busy hysteria lathered on burnt toast

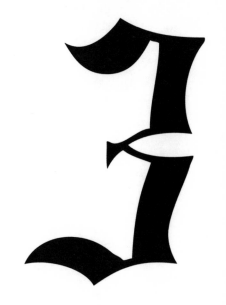

Gibberish —

Ronnie's Gibberish

Scream.   Royal   sighs.
        Oh, Butterfly, in my dark blue sky. Head twitch. Muted fight.
                Unspoken itch.   Fiending.   Best believing.
Dog   like   behaviour,   you,
my saviour and my catalyst to my smooth and self soothing
behaviours.   See ya later.
My world is clouded, red and blue.
Butterfly came about, good news was new.

                        Lazy and crazed. Silly faces, jacked up traces,
                the marks that conjures 30 remarks on your past endeavours.

                            'What happened?'
                                    "How did you do it"?
            Scars.   Dazed.
                          Lost Days.

                My best effort left me.   93
                The beauty in the hurt of the mate that you carry.

You're fucking spunked.. I'm on my fucking larry.

                    Candle lit room,
            30 meerkat heads and I'm merely at my dreamt of edge.
                                So what's your pledge?
I'm sober with nowt, just little doubt and 30 snouts.
        Americans say rowte.   We say route.
The   English.   Oh,   The   English.

Butterfly I do try.
Torn up feet, you make me fleat.
                    Blood sizzles in London's heat, with your flight,
                                I am pleased to retreat.
    Unsubtle ease just when eyes tease.
                        Butterfly,   pollen tricken.
                    My Hayfever,   My Butterfly.
                            I'm a sneezer. Fucking drunk larry.
Sadly, I'm fiending, yet never needing.
                    30 turning heads.

606 Gibberish

Let's wait for Jack.
In the height of July,   it's been 16 months since I've been fucking high.
My reply to unbothered love,

crack.
A lady who doesn't love me back.
I do try,   I'm here in July.
All wet and secretly dry.
   That's half of my lie.
My truth,
   held through flags on some cunt's roof and old hags I fantasise over,
                    that I'm loose.

Seemingly soft in a pantsy affair of all that is anti towards the success of love.
                    With a burden of a boys pain.
Where the cunting fuck is Jack.
          Soft whiskey in the next life's dream,
                    rich as the next,
                    put down like ripped up jeans.
Medicine for self,
          piano keys,
          pictures through sound from imagination for half the world to see.
Jack's here now   in his dressing gown.
                    He lifts my frown.
                                        That lovely face.
If you follow my feet in the search of joy,   you will pull the fool up in me.
Wherever Me and Jack are placed, rufty tufty,
          everything else in the room seems to dagger us, with a rush of distaste.

I pear back to when the world half loved me.   I cannot see what's above me.

I sit beside 2 lovers.
Fingertips on fingertips.
Cradled.
No.

15 Stops Gibberish
Notting Hill to Leyton

Pause all things ampt
The train is veering off course
The   tickling   mischief   that   occurs
From a dodgy verse
Within a newly addressed tune Brainwashes monkeys

As they evolve

Stealing dignity   95
And love throughout

This train sung chaos
Through its horn
The course was in all
How the train was torn

Not in the

Lavish designs and mangled interior Often commuters

Never find comfort
In a literal pack of sardines
Welcoming aliens sweat just to get home

Ronnies Gibberish 2

Sweetened itchy palms

Like when the opiates are yelling at my soul I'm free as a bird
Crouched

Plotting
Nearly whole

The bass presses
And all I've pent up

Lessens

Me and my scraggly vest
Chewed up gracefully by Ronnies

Deep red

Im invited on an appeasing quest
Ink over led

Wait

Scrap that
I'd do anything to manipulate

My dread
Frozen

Married to the sensation of warm water trickling over uncertainty
Shenanigans of love

Run through Soho

Zig zagging with a mishap
Each room is cold
Same as her lap
In which I fold

I informed her to meet me on the flipside Where my switch
From major to minor
Is a little less snide

Where I could say

I acquaint with Mr Jekyll and Mr Hyde

606 Gibberish *2*

Last time I was here I got mugged by 3 little Weans Pesky Cunts.

Hoping to not get snuffed this time round.
These fuckas are ever so naive with a reckless hunger to claw at
anything like I'm some desolated runt. Behind the lady in front,
couples, all ages, show varied faces like personalities in cages.

Chosen claps.

The waiters fif faff accompanied by the sweet mania of jazz.
Stunted chat.

My mind dormant like a resting bat.

The piano pitta patts and a distant heart drifts back.

It ain't exactly necessarily so...   If I wasn't here, my head would stoop
so so low.

It's always near.

Like sweat it only comes to show.

It being, it. No poignant word can scribble a picture for your noggin.

For it, has nowt to admit.

So I sit.

It's always, it.

Ain't Nothing but Blues Gibberish

She wants me to act a fool

She wants 14 of my love poems
that were written on the paper that i used to wipe my arse
When certain things were of more importance
than buying toilet roll
She wants soggy tissues

She wants me to filter my honesty
when it comes to the good and true words i have for her
She wants me to arrive after dinner

She wants me to call her tragic things
She wants me to know how much she hates herself and anything that
tickles her core She wants to dance with me on the window sill
She wants to love me till death is the last drill
She wants half of whatever I've got
She wants painkillers on a monday morning

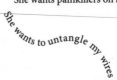

She wants to untangle my wires

She wants to know how to kill hate with desire
She wants brown
She wants a sledge hammer
She wants kisses that gather
She wants stale custard creams
She wants her end on a merry go round

She wants to feel her tragedy suck her beauty dry
with all that it is she wants
She wants dot dot dot

Dwindling with the Boujee (Petit Armitage Hotel Gibberish)

Play it cool
In this room
Charlie showcases himself through lively jawlines And eyeing marbles
Spinning pretentious gifts
Manipulation through one whisper

One sniff
The world shifts
Pass me your nostrils
Candle light flickers
The LA accent reoccurs some nagging bicker
So it seems
Here a London boy is less of a Mister
So it seems
Get a load of it

Toasted by ego

The wallpaper shriveled like the souls
In this laughing stock of a place
Behind the numbing
Of each hidden face

Vagabond Gibberish

Cramps.

Sunnies on.

Shielded from all that seems to approach me.

Hampstead Heath station.

Dried flem from the sprout of the mornings gob.

Look at a passerby and tell them 'hi' with your eyes.

Dogs whine through the lack of receiving a heed..

Selfishness must leed through a raised chin.

Tilted with warped pride, strides that initiate cramp.

The moneyless fine of shame,

through a disgusted glare like unspoken blame,

inflicted through a stare.

Hard butter is not fair.

Leave me where there is little sun,

where no dogs can run and where I am the only one.

Absent from others wishes.

Responsibility stimulates life with a couple more dishes to wash.

Just pray,

I double my lot,

before in living,

I am lost.

Covent Garden station.   Piccadilly line.

My day has progressed.

The luxury of seeing a rat scurry on

the underground hasn't become.

Luxuries have burdens.

Telling the less fortunate one.

As I warm my seat on this tube.

I wear my sunglasses, still.

Little light intrudes and smitten prudes lose.

Cafe Boheme Gibberish

Sir,
      You spilt your pea soup...
Now
      How to recoup?
Chitta chatta
      Do you want this touch
        In tatters
        Maltreated
      Or does it not really matter?
Finger the Defeatists
Snide pricks
Pitta   patta
Attention   scatters
Friday   afternoon
        SoHo
Chaplin   walks
Muted   talks
     Your eyes a no go
Here in SoHo
Little really know
    Crude endeavours flow Pea soup
        Gloopy
        Droopy
Life in a loop
With a crook
           I'd rather go

La Grainne Cafe
Gibberish

New York,

You have viscously spoilt me throughout the years
The same old junkie's inventory spilled out on Lucien's fine veneer
Should wooden dining cut it
For my expectations of majestic self implosion
With the whores buzzing

The sores moaning
And the weirdness of habitual loading phoning
Dirt and grit the twins of twilight beauty
And the daughters of pain's mutiny
New York sure holds it
My heart sure loads it
Tables enable me
The city hums hymns of broken realities
Stagnant blackouts
Forgotten whereabouts
New York has a homely unstated shadow
Deserving of an exposing shout out
Washington square park

Crisp cold sharpens
Humans scamper and beetle
Humans work, burp, hurt and lurk to beg for their sought after steeple
No one can be equal
Sweet tooths stately ungrateful after a wolfish sickly smooch
We all take our best loot and consume further
Unwholesomely ill
Unsatisfied before we inject our best try

Tell a lie
Needles pry
In living I cannot pause to cry
City life gobbles me up
I'm guessing also for the next man
Downers act as my fan
New York
Many thanks
Kisses
Hugs
Nose rubs and all of the rest
New york you're the best
You put me to very own test

Smalls Gibberish

Leaning on you

The click of a finger

Treasured touches to mingle
This room nears happy

Ohhhhh Sally!

Silently howling through a grin
Hounding feelings to repent
The scream of the trumpet

And my blood thins
The blues lie to me outside of this room

Ohhhhh Sally!

Tonight our ears treated with the giving cries of Jazz Us,
Synchronized spies
Devouring each note to settle our gluttony
Hindered by expectations
Drowning in limitations

In this room

We float

Ohhhhhh Sally!

In this seat I sink
Melting on the realisation of gathered momentary bliss To rethink

Ohhhhhh Sally!

I sink
Bottles wink at me with absolutely no caution

Avalanches of fascination
Batter me all through this autumn
Here in smalls
Me and You
Strung out delicately across the beaten walls
By the buzzing
Guzzling
Most loving sounds that are pressed
With leaping hearts to mounds
And pounds of melodious tissues 105

Arresting any of our carried issues Just in this room
Ohhhhhh Sally...

606 Gibberish *3*

Rickety placement of hands
                    Yelling enrollments of gauges for hearts tinkles
            Writing in riddles ceases to solve my trouble with connection
            I wonder what she's reckoning?

                                        7 coffees and its 9:56PM

            When will dread shake my hand?
            Anything becomes excessive when your mate
                        Blue dilutes the days plans

What is minute when Mr More takes your boring self on a tour?
                    Tonight's dinner nears splendid
Cracking without a sight or an ear on what's even happening
                        Just warped tasted
                        Buckled necessities shape me
                        Haste tied to thoughts
Flirts to mislead my concrete greedy needs
                                    Up her sleeve was another mister

        An increased intake of blues
        The camel rests on my back
        Sonny deceased
        Sally elevated

                                            Thoughts
                                            Pipes
                                    Distort hoped heights

                    Strenuous nights
Remorse within the course of love
After I've completed all of the above Trench coats

Heistful blokes

                              I'll never choke

Unless the rope
Which hasn't passed on it's note
                    Gets at my throat
                    For now I'm afloat
Thoughts
    Perfect tarts always had my intrigue
As did pained souls
Prolonged tolls
And
That head you just can't rid
                              Embittered dessert
                              Nutella cheesecake
A trumpet and a familiar hurt
Claps with wooos
Eye sex with a third of a clue
                    Dirt sprung
                    My third leg is hung
                    Bite ya tongue
                    Missy spun
                    To run or cum

                              Mysteries intrude
                              Like a prude
I've lost the grasp on my best loot
I want love just like that

13 Stops Gibberish Kensal Green to Embankment

Paper   boy
>   Announce the delivery
>   So the deliverer can deliver the delivery

Not   you
>   Inform the informer
>   So many sincere whispers float
>   Intendingly to a misplaced receiver
>   Dusty bakerloo line carriage

Nippy   wind
>   Just me and a hardened Londoner
>   Eyeing up the only newspaper

Between   us
>   See ya later

Smudged   ink
>   Do not flinch
>   You may get battered

Swallowed   up
Chewed   up
>   Ravaged
Spat   out
>   Even if you seemingly manage
>   I'd rather die sideways
>   No staple speaks to longevity
>   Darts fly with sighs

And   somewhere
>   There is always blood and piss in the snow
>   Only midget and midget like things know

Deja   vu   limbo
>   Stamp on the scarecrow
>   Kiss the black crow

Death   in   love

Death   in   dust
                Most people skip around naively
            While injustice chores a ride off ya back
Take   me   downstairs
                To the cradle of sincerity
Permanent   naps
                    But don't let me go
                    Do not let me go
                    Downstairs
On   my   lonely
                Whisper wicked needs
                If only we were to receive
The   cutting   deeds
            That lurk below the reeves
            Up a armless mans sleeve
        One day I will happily forget to breathe
            Howling rebellion has become

Runaway   Son

                                                    Heroin swayed Mum

                        The day after heartbreak won

                        A perfumed empathetic girl licked my bum

Maida   Vale

    Newspaper readers are more respectable than telephone scrollers

Motorola   legend

Innocent   blowers

            Whoever locates my Dad will get granted £927,000,000

                                                            Promise

                        Just so I can spit in his face

        Tell me where sweetness is brewed with the uppermost affection

                        Sell me your charm

                        Sell me your subtle ways to harm

Your   scandalous   luck

Your   weakest   arm

                        And I'll chop off my strongest

                                    Promise

                    I will never step foot in Richmond again

                    Lea resides there

                    Right by the river

                    She gives her eyes with emptiness to the Thames

As she droopingly plots her limbs slenderly like a happily dying flower

                    She knows in her right wicked heart

                    that she paid off all of the dominos

                                                        We all know

                                                They all fell but one

                        See it

                        Say it

                        Solve it

Tell me what my own life means

Skanky Truth —

Who Owns Truth?

I have crossed the pond to Los Angeles
For 3 nights of pressing a pen
Words tend to rape me of my, my, my...
Wordsmiths do not exist
Wordsmiths if ever
Are just fools fooling fools
Cleverly
I don't think so
Poets exist only behind the wine cellar door
A Poet is one questioning all
A Poet is a dweller
Cautiously searching for the fruits of existing
While welled to last decades door
A Poet is just another
Tom, Dick or Harry
Sally, Lizzy or Crissy
Unaware of their real name
Their own calling
Only their downfall
And the pier in which darkness is mooring

Paranoia on the Hills of Los Angeles

Cradled within the squelch of the devil's thighs
Palm trees tower wisely
Dry dirt swept by gentle winds
Parched smirks
Battles with Los Angeles' heat
With out of mind defeat
Jealousy creeps
After proud footsteps
That stride somehow neatly neat
The angered glimmer of the city
Penetrates me
Openly
As I run so slowly
Closing shop
Midday
The spite of yesterday's movement
Prized to be bagged up in mass today
London is distant
So is water
So is any reminiscence of an angel
Gifts
Rewards
Escapes
Choosing clarity clouded by joy
This city is some kind of ploy
My relationship with skies that leak blue
Only horns sounds of spoken tongues
Of all I wish I knew
When the curious one yells for half a clue
Only dust swirls off disregarded essay papers
Dialogues of see ya laters

But really steel like goodbyes
Left with only dust
As the lonely tracer

Moistures distant
So is untampered reality
So is my box of things
Psychosis chose this hocus pocus

It is mysterious and magical
How the world chooses to prize me
And how the world intrusively blabbers
Last tipped by rubber lips
That are undertaken with blue tints
Mythic madness shat out of life's asshole
Smelling crisp
Life's beauty
Battered by Life's lisp

Kicking the Bucket

Eternal rest is the end
Once I hold what loves me best
I'm an overplayed tune that still longs
To be noticed
In the ways that I misbehave
Death is hungry for me
Deaths nook is my destiny
Once what I hold
Loves the rest of me

All for the Appreciative

I'm a wishy washy young man
You can get the job done with me
Slippery with a forgiving threshold for all that's appreciated

"Please"
Course, I'm polite. Far from tight. But I'll treat ya just right

"Sex?"
If needs be, I could be tickled by guilt, if I don't love her
So, only with my adored one

"Eye Contact?"
I do try my very best. With one, eyes can be an antidote

"Sadness?"
Animals get down
I'm ok
As long as she
As long as I'm out of my dressing gown by 10:30

"Sports?"
Cycling round London, sure does fit
Football on a Wednesday, sure goes sick
Sooooooo... Mmm Yeah

"How about ya Lady?"
How so shady?

I'll withdraw now.
Thanks for your appreciation.
Just, please...
have a real gander
before this matter rolls off your fucking tongue

Learning to Swim Should be a Sin

— Sonny Hall and Ahmed Alramly reverb

Camels and a red rose
Gentle snakes and tattered toes
Smashed wedding cakes in rows
Repeated mistakes
High stakes
Wine stained clothes
Welcomed insanity grows
Dampened vanity shows
Bloody moons for the lows
And my star woes
Only this tale can know
Disturbing muck
Through this love I cluck
Through this world I'm stuck
Pride tucked for the awaiting judge
Fate outlucked
Life like a rake
I'm tediously plucked

Torn
Pricked by a thorn
When love blows my horn
Mum's tear because i'm near
And I can see but I can't hear
My internal brawl
I brake to stall
I fall
At the table for all or nothing
Of course I called
Pub huddles
Are my nearest cuddles
An isolated snuggle
The bliss I chase
The empty gas station

The golden pool
Is the petrol puddle of fools
Love blinds my tools
Like a pen poor of ink
In you pool
I sink with the bottle I richly drink
For pink I'm blue
The lives and lies we choose
Through a grafted disguise
I'll lose
With you
Pink skies loom
Behind me
Hidden cries
And a trusted demise
Soon

What's a swim without a wave?
What's a cave without a light?
What's a path without a twist?
What's a hero without a myth?

For all I've missed
I find the crisp in life
Crunched
Poisoned
Resented like a school lunch
Yet at first
All was presented like roses in a bunch
I long for a normal day
Raining with clouds grey
Before my will led me astray

I try to swim
Dry like hay
Stained by pain
Day to day
I stare at the dryer tumbling If I jump in
Will I spin anew
Or will all my stains turn all those whites
Blue

Head Bruiser

Like a fly head butting a window
I am trying to get out
Escaping one's own trickery
Belittling life's senseless creed
Slipping soft whiskey in my morning tea
With crooked ladies, sour ladies and lovely ladies
And half the heart i started off with
Ducking and diving any right parallel
With limited fun that lives only in faulty elevators
And in car parks that have no space for me
And that fucker who has never owned a car who finds himself in this
car park standing next to me
And that group of waxed saints who have a sincere lust for life
And those raving environmental activists that sniff a gram of coke
twice or three times a week
And the handy noose seller
And the dizzy maybe too self aware teen girl who is struggling to
breathe after running 2 kilometres
On a rainy monday morning
She is scared that her lungs will cave in
and her own heart give up on her
But she will do it again on Wednesday
And Friday
And Sunday
And then all over again
Because she has to look tip top for the lads
And for the creme de la creme courthouse that is our earth
I remain observant

Not nosey
Hunting for a boundless membership
Like fake eccentrics who inquire with psychiatrists
about their madness
Like the supposedly shaken artists who are ever so scared of dying
Like a homoesexual man passionately licking an ice lolly on Old
Compton Street in the winter time
It is incredible when you depict the world's happiness
And sadly
Provokingly seductive when you depict the world's madness
Lean on a pension of infinite smiles
Or practice your loving vows for disaster itself
Whatever situation i stick my finger into
I am still head butting a window

Missing my Loved Ones that went Missing

— Forever

My loved ones are dropping dead
My loved ones are slow dancing with hurt
Lovers die but then self fixing fixation prys and then new lovers arise
But when my loved ones drop dead
I only see nagging bullseyes on every existing randomers face
walking down the street
I'd punch you, you and you and probably you
If you didn't make me wanna screw your face with the tippity tip of my shoe
I catch myself walking like Charlie Chaplin and Charlie's got a dodgy
leg and he's smoking crystal meth
and 19 spanish bulls are chasing him down the Ladbroke Grove
Hopingly stashing grief in 105 hugs while I drench many shoulders
with tears that drip from my closing curtains
My left shoulder is drenched
So is my right
So is yours
So is hers
We may as well all cry and all take a communal shower
And clean ourselves from tragedies lively shock
The air smells like my dead mates
The coffee tastes like my dead mates
I can only dream about my dead mates
When I eat my stomach twists as if my dead mates are in there trying to
resist the preconceived gist of life's pre written death list

We can hope on love

Beholding thin Skin

Scars leathered with distaste of self
The skin of the beholder bleeds
The lark of destructive needs breeds
Her scars sown with his
Children left on the bottom shelf
Pain styled as a brew
With a remarkable fizz
Cutting gone wild
Sizzle
Drizzle
Blood kindles
And drips
The skin of the beholder
Dread kissed
She may need a resting kip
In her own skin she bloody drifts

The Thing that Killed my Mum

I owe myself room for a cared for vessel
Nestled below my brain
Chiseled above my heart
One of such where loneliness is smart pain
Like shooting darts
And life like a game only seen in the dark
The thing that killed my Mum
Seems far from fun
Yet an easy one to fasten my escapist run
Or at least something to ease all I feel
When I'm hung

Ya see
Balance comes with disgruntlement
For the unsatisfied one
Like my Mum
I wonder what it is I carry
Sickness can rally
While close calls tally
I find comfort in the next darling Sally
When sadly
It is only one darling I dare
Or care to carry

This entry is the nuts and bolts of it
The tedious cutthroat stuff
That jolts and pokes my insides
As I try and revolt priceless baggage

The thing that killed my Mum
Could make a snare drum numb
Could dumbfound anyone
With the brief bliss that becomes

Sharply nipping this afternoon's hurt in the bud
Just for this afternoon
Because all that we feel comes too soon
This thing is like air to a balloon
With crooks
The misunderstood
The stood on
And lovers that got forgotten
Before the Nitty
Was innocence in turmoil
And love from the bottom
Ever so rotten

Some were just the ones rich with it
Yet fastly trod on
It had already begun
The thing that killed my Mum

My Mum
Pained
Ashamed
Her imagination like a train stopping through many stations
Disengaged
Full of love
Riddled through every engagement
Abandoned liaisons left my Mum
In that things basement

I still want a taste of that thing
To bury myself for a second
So I can wonder where I've been
A taste for a waster is what I reckon
After my love is beckoned
A waster

If my darling scraps me
Lost in the wind
Still besotted with less of a grin
I'd choose London's finest gin
And gathered saliva to swallow my favoured pill
A waster
If
A waster with my best belief
These things go on
Until
That thing has me strong
It's in all that's underneath
                    The thing that killed my Mum

Wash Your Hands

Like his empty bottle of wine
He wonders where she's gone
Like a penny that's lost its shine
He continues to get passed on

A Tactile Destiny

I like it when she sucks my cock
The closeness between life and death
Has never looked this close
The real beauty in things is when
There is absolutely nothing in between
Poetry makes it all alright
She likes it when i bow down
With my head in between her legs
And i show her that i really love her
Maybe i love forgetting for a little while
When i plonked my bum on this seat
I felt like this poem would be a real masterpiece
But the head is a tricky cunt
Life is a big old ploy
I want to expose myself and everyone else
Because realness is really lacking
And i haven't even seen an eighth of this planet
Maybe realness hides elsewhere
Or maybe my openness is slacking
In the end rubbish always takes the win
And
Profound sadness always seems to overrule the genius
The liars get the golden ticket
And honest humans dissolve in distrust
Gagging madness flipping the coin
Show me to the jagged rust
Dear Death
Let me join
An untreated tetanus infection must host a slow dismissal
Right?
She likes it when im lying about my lust for life
And my lust for her

Love was always just a cold cup of tea to stir
Awkwardness makes us do strange things
I didn't even know my heel was jabbing at the floorboard
When i notice it in others
I peer into their soul like i've found bundles of gold
Maybe if we understood more
Life would be somewhat easier to control
I hope that your existence is a trustworthy one
Days skip by like wildfires
Days leave us like breaths
Days spree by like survival tests
Could you manipulate your day to treat you just right?
The right people
The right food
The right coffee with the right cigarette
The right sex and the right work
The right absurdities to make you chuckle through all of the hurt
Keep us here
As long as all the cats and dogs are trusting in the state of this world
Once that goes astray
Do not dare ask me to stay

An alcoholic Fright on a December Evening in Kensal Rise

Mr 70 Centilitre Bottle of Appleton Rum
Please may you let me be
I've met stranger's eyes that respectfully measure their stare
More cautiously than you
Annexing glassy prick
You are just an old mate
That is all...

One man could

My thoughts could create one man
My thoughts could distill one man
My thoughts could free one man
My thoughts could seize one man
My thoughts could kill one man
My thoughts, thought about that one man
And
I thought why to call him one man
When that one man...

Is me.

Unhappy Endings

Today
I saw every emotion that ever flapped through Baker street
Sad ideas
Peacock colours injected into London's marching intellect

I looked at Baker Street with resigned eyes
Baker street looked at me
Showcasing monkey vessels and searching desperate respect
Baker street told me something
and i told Baker Street something back
Me and the human race already lost our heads
But i never thought to feel empathy for the others
Or myself
Who died for who?
Massage parlour Baker Street
Your throbbing bellend died for you
Some Chinese lady
Some soul sucking
Better for nutting
Seduction machine
Thousands of likely babies died for what?
Forty quid and she had to do it 15 times
again today just to feed the kids
Scream the shady basement announcement
For this newly made sket queen mother
Slimey spunked oily cheques
Vomiting flies grip the walls

Tonight the family dinner table is rather fruitful
Meaningless sperm clamped by half cleaned red towels
If flies threw up would we even be able to see their sick?
We all have to do what we have to do
To do what we want to do or do not want to do
In order to just do
Read the lines above for life's tip off
Snide smug cunt
Baker Street
Marylebone road
Picture a buck toothed dazzler prancing around on the street corner
Singing Chet Baker with 60 pence in his cup
I'd die of choking on a mushy banana before i am pleased
Especially after today's run of shameful get arounds
Take my heart and bleach it in a room of crystals and stones
And burning forgiving sage
No one has died yet
But we need to know who dies for who and who dies for what
Otherwise aimless self dismantling
Is a lot for us confused stragglers
The one girl i ever loved told me to die for her
I'd die by the spell of love
Not by the truth of it
I'd do it in a hotel suite at the Bulgari
Because taste would have left me by the time
I acted on any defeating thought

Will we Live to
Remember this?

— Paris

Pen borrower
You are never getting that back
Peace of mind stealer
Slumped in the 10th Arrondissement
Confiding in my borrowed pen
Desperate misdemeanour
Let me tell you that you are never getting that back
The loneliest of men resent love but it's the only thing that they need
You'll never get back what you put in the bin
Wash your filthy hands please
My world stops when i meet the gypsy lady's plee
Let me tell you never please a charmer
Tennis ball glands but you'll still kiss me
Kamikaze attacks 0.3 kilometres from our love cocoon
Why do all these men want to kill themselves just to greatly rubbish
my only love?
Punished adulation
How did that man lose his left leg?
I'm lonelier than him and i can walk
And love
And fuck
Maybe he is one of those love slewing kamikaze survivors
Living with the best of the worst luck
It's 12 minutes past midnight in Paris
I'm three quarters drunk soaking in some vacant cadence
City's bloom in the hours when only the greatest minds are present
I'm not calling myself one of the greatest's
I have 4 hours to go
And I'll probably be blackout by then

Many sit with the Wish to be Noticed By Millions

Popping wobbly popularity muncher
Sellotape fiddling celebrity
Losing breath for words to tell the next man
Suffocating under gypsy stardom
Who is that popular fella?
What's the coated intention behind the loudmouth storyteller?

What's the angle?
What's the price of wickedly proportioned attention?
Fame whore diva pleading to be the leader
Youthful days of preying on Madonna
Fucked your mad skull into a skewed pirated demeanor Sucker
punched in the gut by artful Hollywood cocksuckers
Sweating bloody insecurities to relish into slewed dreams
You are the fucker that fucks the one standing on the stand
The fucker that other fuckers that like standing strong, stand on
In the back of Bar Italia
I see you perched cross legged
Irritated
Brooding while slurping a Negroni
Wedgied by incessant phoneys
Showcasing your lasting sad face
Waiting on the world to exhale a dear epiphany
Like a lightning bolt shock realization
Threating it's finally found awareness of you
You think to be the lad
That one prolific day
You'll make the world so so glad

I have learnt that the Chicest of People are the Most Crooked

She said "Sonny you should know that you are very special, take this as a great privilege. Me, sucking your cock. I haven't touched another cock seperate from my husbands, in 15 years"
No ambition is false or wrong but desire can be sickly
and I know that the best part of any silent delight is the all alone
cab drive to the unassured unhinged unavailable practically all
bounds unknown lady
Or the tube hop to the bag of coke
Or the motion of knocking at that persons door for your box of pills
Or the extended split second before the first punch
Or the buying and selling of your own lust but only before you bust
The anticipation of executing urged devotion
The rich get desirables nippier than the rest of us
They are deprived of the thrilling graft that leads to any kind of
sleazy sweet stuff
So they then have to heighten the grime of any sleazy sweet stuff
that they want to indulge in to feel that
Sweet icky feeling
Weaknesses sigh
I'm not rich and never was
But I flutter with the rich and learn from the rich
Observing the rich and all the horribly rich mistakes
that the rich make
I remain searching London and elsewhere for the ultimate
silent delight
Only really enjoying the eve of each

Telling Fibs
Would not Make Sense
at this Point

This is a toned down note
To my last seen 16 years ago Dad
To my future lover
To the fella I get my coffee from every morning
Who has seen every bound of me
Yet doesn't know me at all

All I want to do

— Tightrope Realisations
on April 23rd 2019

A purer man when pushing my pen
An unalloyed man when making mucky love to my typewriter
When i step away from the breeziness of english language
The world comes to me
Like Obese New Yorkers at lunchtime
stomping on freshly laid snow to get to the hot dog van
The world comes to me
Like a gunky fever greeting the bride on her wedding day
The world comes to me
Like the 3rd day of existing for the junkie departing from his only
concrete love
The world comes to me
Like fireworks attacking a sleeping sky
The world comes to me
Like a cumshot from any throbbing cock
The world comes to me
Like a shameless name drop
The world comes to me
Like lightning in Venezuela
Like sunshine in Los Angeles
Like October rain thumping on the crowns of tourists in London
The world comes to me
Like suicide in a happy family
Like crackheads greeting actuality
Like the first meddlesome thought of the day

The world comes to me
Like milk transforming tea
The world comes to me
Like a pointless frenzy
The world comes to me
Like trusted food on a belemics plate
Like a vegan being force fed black pudding as no mistake
The world comes to me
Like the result of placing your happiness in someone else
The world comes to me
Like performing a U-turn driving a limousine
The world comes to me
Like a half remembered dream
The world comes to me
Like an earthquake during the purest of honeymoon sex
The world comes to me
Like sensitivity stroking bedlam
The world comes to me
Like a lump to a hypochondriac

Like making sense of a maniac
Like a snail lost on the railroad tracks
The world comes to me
Like anxiety on your snuggly pillow
Like profanity on the dinner table
The world comes to me
Like the world comes to you
The world comes to me
Like living without a clue
A purer man when pushing my pen
But if i was always as pure as them
As pure as then
When pushing my pen
There would be no room for bonding with reality
Mingling with loose heads
Up together heads
Human beings living as rock stars instead
Human beings morphing into pillheads
Human beings acting like they are alright at best
Human beings locked up in bed
Stale bread vessels hoping on postponed mortality
Naked truth in feelings
Sightings
Hearings
Please dear World
Inject me with some reality again
All i want to do is to reside in my pen

Where does this all go?

It would be sad to mould every given moment
Into some immortal pleasing jiffy
I'm tired of pinching at happiness
Short of breath
I'm far too empathetic to that all alone old man
Sitting longingly
Fantasising over his dead wife's ghostly presence
I'm far too kind to that waitress
Who serves pricks like me all year long
I'm far too wishful
Wishing on a happy medium for some kind of constant unity
Snippets of attachments float by
Like egocentric notoriety on the 13th floor of any corporate shithole
Notice that your dreamy brain is violently aware
that you could just jump
Acknowledgment does go a long way
When you are present
to feel the truth in the length of a shared split second

Fondling With
my Inked up Doll

Sometimes I think to write a poem
When...
I'm glossing my lips with yours
When...
I'm doing obscure things that'll raise an eyebrow or two
Runner
Double up
Stakes
Maneuvering
Limp handshakes
A head nod
A dear chap
Who even pays for the cunting tube?

Women know how to somewhat...
Somehow be my lubricant for living
A third of the time

Anyway, to write for me, is a need...
Like brushing my teeth
Or loving one
Or even wiping my bum
I need to tamper with what's beneath
Otherwise, I'd find myself grinding my teeth
Turning a questionable leaf
And then...
It'll be the ground
I'll be beneath

If I could

I don't ask any walking sweetness
Or anyone matter of fact
For the case of true wellbeing
Or to unravel any given nuisance
I chase to hold ice
Do not fight for me
No matter what night it may be
If I could cry
I'd maybe weigh less
If I was a lady
I'd definitely flaunt a dress
The norm of living with distress
The load of reading through little words
But plenty mess
I don't ask

Heightened Tingles
Somehow always
Locate me

Imagine the thrill of knowing an assassin is coming for you
And your loved one
He holds 3 guns
7 knives
One that is rather long
A grenade
And chopsticks to poke up your bum
Imagine the thrill of knowing an assassin is coming for you
And your loved one
Cuffed to adrenalin
Highs with a known ending
Always tend to initiate the next one

Where is the pleasant whirlwind?
That wretches my adam's apple
Down to my belly button
Then shreds apart the whole thing
Thrusting my adam's apple through my wrinkled skin
Forcing me to frantically fasten up my birth button

Life is cold
Life is wondrous
The circus always finds me
I've only taken 9 Vicodin today
The valium doesn't count anymore
World war 3 shells inside and out

Just today I have toured the whole of europe with the circus

The Assassin is coming
And I cannot be in one place for more than 14 minutes

Tender pillow strangle me to an indefinite snooze
Droopy universe hijack the nasty stuff from the serpentine hands of
madness Loopy maniacs take a bow

Praying for a hit of something
A hit of something
A hit of nowt
Nothing
A hit of the feeling when a dying flower
gets soaked with water and sun
A hit of murderous fun
A hit of 523 men cumming at once
A hit of something
Praying for a hit
A hit of life's skewed anatomy
I want to buy a house on the hill
In the nook of genius insanity
And be blackened
Scorched on my tip toes
Breaking through the satisfying sting of a high
It's another pill but for me it's everything

Sorry Spider

In the toilet
Long legs
Trying
Abiding and deceiving
Long stretched
Deserving of a holy grail
Free of a crucifying nail
Heiving
I find myself short from receiving
Dormant and teasing
Demonic scampers distract the needy
Detering all I picture that is second to me
Alluring the skatty
Retracting disused spanners
While acting activists spread their dated banners
Raving delirium

Sorry Spider
I just adore your merry scutter
By fair means
I staple to write
For you conjure my dishonourable stutter
Smitten with greens
Heinous words can trickle out from common mouths
As if your highness ever swayed proper clouds
The word special gets thrown around
Words bruised and disused
I'm continuously and tediously
Flipped
Green to blue
And Spider I may be true
I did find you
By my loo

The Looking Glass
always Cracks

I remember the last time seeing my Mother
All the knife and forks
On our table were the wrong way round
Covent Garden sung paranoia
Through the eyes of shared blood
I soon became all that I saw that day

Some Greedy Lady
Some Lost Boy
a Pen, my Moleskine
Lust and Envy

Tie my shoelaces and wrestle with my shaft
While I bathe in camel cigarettes
Clouded by barren notions
You, my feeble ocean
Curlilocks, I'm ever so lost
Your breasts mulling over my moleskine
While my sliced hands fly desperately over the page
And then shammingly to your cracking solemn face
Just trying to be fair
Just trying to flee all that's really there
Hell is nice but only with your heavenly slice
Ease is no treat
Love neat
Repulses me
Skin my soul like an onion
Then let me exploit your eyes
You're the flush on my vacant flesh
And your love is the blood shedding catalyst
Bashful about its very own request
The tester
The spat on jester
And the insensitive mist
Cursed with a winking wanking ravishing twist
Bring the plasters
Seek the masters of decoding broken biological urge
Fantasys purge
Dogs of self loathing
And the makers of bacterias banishing soap
In our chasm
We are suspended

A Note to Someone Who is Sometimes Somewhat Similar to Me

You sick fucking pencil basher
Sharpen your empathy
Before you polish over your faked harmony of living
Kisses turn giddy
Replacing meaning
And human like word ping pong
You love sick fucking pencil basher
Walking piece of pasta
Listless
Blissless
Torment Landlord
Lost Mister
Shy of a good quality working pen
Each kiss is asking you with strangled sympathy
What happened to you?
And when?

Inking Shy Petals

Masturbation flanked by the jitter of some pen

> Who gets forgotten?

> Who strikes a chord upon a saving deed?

The strawberries were always rotting

Skins pores open and close

Hot n' cold

Shyness

Inhibited shrinking rested on the shoulder of any mess

Think to mention

The poor stinging lady

> Who said shyness?

Extract distress

But how?

The red wine already canoodled with her white dress

Monkey man

Saving grace

> How could any man utter less?

Strapping and hefty

Can we get this man a fucking vigorous virgin mary?

> Please?

> A formidable virgin man?

> Who said shyness?

Back breaker

Tax taker

The one you shall see later

There is no pen here for when this one runs out

Darkness tickles death

Life charges a penny per breath

Death

Shyness

Soft close to cashmere

Yet brittle like an early ones untimely tear

Life

Shyness

Nowt to muster

Just a new pen

And one less to care for

Accumulating a Trying ill Will

Jellyfish with spells of love
5 snapped toes
2 Atheists
And a map to Bethlehem
1 broken pen
A fatigued hand
Jellyfish sting ointment
And a tutorial on how to smile
A world to walk over
93 billion cars
Pent up feelings
19 generations of trauma
A kleptomaniac son
A whoring daughter
Complaints
Followed by restraints
And 4 scowling south London boys
42 minutes till landing
I've never wanted to comedown this much
1 working pen
100 working men
3 blind gamblers
101 working ladies
Absent parents
Morning perspiration
The day's only sweetness
Los Angeles calls
New highs
Concrete lies
7 mates hiding a bag of what not
And I walk around with visible snot
The day robots become a thing
I will permanently leave
Zero goodbyes
The rest rots

What a Cunt

The fact of the matter
When it comes to mingling hearts
Is clutter with me
Like a ill at ease mutter
That may as well be a stutter
Twitchy silent back and forths
At full tilt
Im forged into a lesser nutter
Women that inform me on their desire
For Little 'uns tumbling around
One ear snoops
While my other side is mumbling in a mound
On the table dresser
Truly and really the truth in the background
Is much realer than all she sees
Maybe certainty
Is little to naked truth
All twenty year old me tastes
Is sourness
Looped and laced with panic
For time misspent is what she sees
In the loaded fork full
Veering to her sewn mouth
Have ya kiddies if ya please
It just means
You won't be loving my seed

For twenty year old me
Has other shite to see
These 2 women
I do adore
I could not flaw
Oh only if I was older
I'd happily snap my fingers
The point being
These ladies doubt their love in me
Like a front line soldier
Sheltering from shots at the rear
Of a nimble tree
Purely because of their
Aging equitable needs

John Pearse does some Good Hats

I once had
A hat that shaped me
It shaped my head even
It rested on my head

Little Little Boy

I have bit my tongue
Fists clenched
Shoulders raised
Someone else's heart in my grasp
While she licked my nipple
Up and down
We remain at the bottom of tomorrow's queue
In line for living's clue
Within my worst remembered places
The Kitchen where Dad battered Mum
And Mine and Harvey's bedroom
Uncatered needy screams
Then in the car
Where I watched from the rear passenger seat
Nightmares dream
I have shut my eyes
Fists clenched
Shoulders raised
My hearts beat rashly squeezed
In someone else's hand
Pissing myself
While disassociation becomes my dearest friend
Hush silly little Boy
Why does water drip from one's eyes?
Little green Boy
Razor like care
Made me the boy willing to dare
Valium sweets
Fuzzy
Luvvy duvvy
Pussy sweat

And you think that this desire is discrete
How many can one eat?
Most days I long for one's tasteful defeat
Me
You
Her
Him
She
Best believe that bruise is a beauty
Here
Blood is the norm
Lady puncher
Soul muncher
Back huncher
Since a boy
Love has been just like the pipe

Loving Pigeons

The thought of killing myself came along once I recognised that
maintaining deformed chivalry was the very definition of my existence
—

I strolled down the Chamberlayne Road
With a lopsided heart
Whispering loose words to the cracks in the pavement
Over my head
The local Pigeons accompanied me
The Pigeons circled each other
Shitting on each other
While telling me they were sick of having each others shit
Matted in each others feathers
The pigeons know far more than me
They know how to have fun
They told me that Sally now lives in Hampstead
In a big old fancy house
And she looks like a sun beam
Desperately trying to find the shadows
My organs are skewed by a stabbing warfare
That has not yet happened
And probably will never happen
As long
As Sally lives joyfully in her quarrel
Of all squabbles
Warming her feet
By her see through gas fireplace in Hampstead

While sobbing pensive machete like tears
Uncovering bad blood
And lost grey love
The Pigeons adore Hampstead
And I appreciate their telling vigilance
However I could cheerfully petrol bomb the entire village

Back to the loneliness of deformed chivalry
Back to the thought of killing myself
Backs to Sally's last pitiful kiss
Back to wishing I would be swallowed up by the cracks in the
pavement just like my shallow words
Back to loving the Pigeons

The Worldly Pigs and Fame and Fortunes Sickness

Nowadays
Casual men and casual women
Casually lunge to pluck plentiful life
From other casual men and casual women
The sky being our shrinking
Overthinking
Stinking ceiling
The sky being our never kneeling
Sometimes healing
Stained collar for how far eyes can see
These sycophantic people
These casual men and casual women
Needs never leave
Needs just plead in the alleys of deceit
In the torn disregarded receipts
Of the food you needn't eat
Pigs and fame
Me and Rodney
Who scrapes through life on his script
Are near to the same
Nowadays
Pigs orally engulf fame from the rear
Then fame flaps and flusters hysteria
Horror within a accurate delight
Fame always finds its desired pig to mould right
Just before midnight

Nowadays
Causal men and casual women are tired
Trapped beneath this sky
Duplicity licks any human being gladly dry
Nowadays
Casual men and casual women ravingly scratch
At the pearly bricks of the opulent walls
Of the castle where the famous pigs live

These Days I Coincide with Aliens every Bleeding Day

I seem to rashly press on the bones of any human being I can get close to
—

These days
It's a myth to dilute reality within a human be
These days
Men n' women gobble up each others sick
For desperate warmth
From the teasing frozen lies
That society's norms squat within
We are all mislaid
Jacked up
So suck it up
Rub it up
Swallow ya known lump
These days
You better
These days
You may as well sow ya lips right shut
Cunting burdens
Hush you sobbing runt
We are all melting in this mut
Where can I find the innocently bleeding day?
Where all the trees swayed our agreeable way

Where even dogs were oblivious to the hurt in our world that day
When and where God was blushing through pleasant acts
Minus the survivors hacks
Minus hates tracks
These days
We are quietly gushing misery's muck
Values seep
Not one lady or man can budge to weep
For it is disgust that we greet
Before eyes pry
Blacked out rooms
And somewhere our forgotten sky
Observing our existence
Heightened by our stifled cries
These days
I rashly press on the bones of any human being I can get close to

For Lea

— 8th February 2018

It never reaches a point of well rounded satisfaction
With anything
The shutter won't shut
And I was told tonight was the night that wrongens will blossom
Open the door for wrong doers
Where is the point that will mould me into the man that smiles freely
and really
To the coffee lady on a glum old morning
The death of numbing shows through raised tension
The life of knowing shows through simply knowing
Knowing the pain of the grey haired man wearing foxy red loafers
at the bus stop
And the sniveling kid
And the bus driver who looks only to his steering wheel as humans
enter his bus
When is the point that meaning is just meaning
And the purposes of purpose aimlessly swims above the concrete line
of wholehearted fulfilment
For heaven's sake let me have all of you
The tippity tip of your lip
The most sensually awake bit of your clit
The smallest smallest slit on your nip
The meek tooth at the back of your mouth
The smile that comes to show
once you know that life's shadow only comes to go
It never reaches a point of well rounded satisfaction
With anything
Is it absurd to be hopelessly scared of the likely gospel
That I will never nip that point
Never grip that point
And to be scared
Of the happenings once that
Truth comes to happen

For Lea
— If I ever have to describe a Specific Warmth

I often wonder if I should end it all
But I'd rather run after you
I've accepted running after you will probably kill me anyway
It never reaches a point of well rounded satisfaction
With anything

I know that you love me
I know how to close the curtains

We are two red and blue helium balloons
Floating above the Embankment bridge
Cowering over all that we know
One Hundred And Forty-Seven catapults stuffed with razor sharp razors
Line up down the Embankment
Licking their rusty lips at the possibility of popping us
Into nothingness
I'd rather die with you
Mangled as one
Floating sideways into a soft spot of portioned hunger

The Worst Investment
I Ever Made

— 26th February 2018

Panic
Panic introduced to every single memory we wrongly birthed
Panic
Panic delighted and smug
An outbreak of shootings
In a shared world longing for bullets to hug
When we first met In New York your sharpness pinched the poisoned
fog from my eyes
Then in Paris we warmed many seats together
while modest devils sat astray
You smoked my insides
Feeding our envious ashtray
Nestled in some nook at Le Select
Our cigarette ash escorted by parisian winds
Our cigarette ash the only thing that will ever leave
Not you
Not you
Then in London we dilly dallied with gathered time
You drizzled me with a lurid lemon and lime
Then in Israel I came to you from London with love to brew
You already knew that this loving conundrum would soon be through
Sourpuss lover

Sentient dread riddled lady
Devoted suicide
Ball squeezing sharp tongued
Herpes spreader
Fabricator intimate devotion blagging storyteller
Eat my led up
I spat on my pencil before writing this poem
after losing unordinary dear love again
Eat my pencil
Pleasure yourself with it
And this poem too
Knowing departure strapping secretly after I fucked all of the love out of you
Panic
The burden of a stubbed out existence still lives with me

Whoever Buys Lottery Tickets Can Take My Place

Say hello to another tragedy
Not just a broken nail
Or a puncture in your bike tyre
Or a leak through your ceiling
This time it's the hole
In your soul that is bleeding
Your soul is like that bloody ceiling
Here comes another tragedy
Another flipping tragedy
Trickling through the cracks in the walls
Soul puncture
Deflated human being
When will you talk?
Because I might
Just
Tell me when my time will be done
So i can say hello to another tragedy
I thought her death was rather tragic
So tell me when is mine?
And how and where?
What about his?
Or hers?
It is all so intriguing
because I don't have a clue what the fuck will happen
And when

Acknowledgments

With Thanks —

Adwoa Aboah	Iris Law	Elliot Long
Sadie Frost	Marley Mackey	Dominic Jones
Joshua Hercules	Max Reginald Robson	Alexander James
Kai Schachter	Ahmed Alramly	Harvey Hall
Jordan Vickors	Domino Leaha	My Mum & Dad
Bakar	Ryan Doyle	Joséphine de La Baume
Nathan Taylor	Federica Pantana	Jim Longden
Jefferson Hack	Mark Herman	Joseff Dorell

A very special thank you to all of my dear friends that have been with me along the many thrills and spills of living, throughout the time I have put this book together. To the ones still here and to the ones that have left us. To Jack Laver my wonderfully talented best friend, for understandingly cracking my words with his telling and shockingly pleasing illustrations. To Rob Meyers, the great unrestrained wizard that put this book together. And to the Cabin Rehab Chiang Mai for helping me out of the stinking quarantined sewers of drug and alcohol addiction and ushering me to write during my rehab process in the summer of 2017.

Text set in Minion Pro Regular, Helvetica Regular, with custom gothic chapter opening fonts